DA BOYZ OF #C74

DA BOYZ OF #C74

RIKERS ISLAND LEGENDZ

BASED ON TRUE EVENTS

FRUITQUAN BAILEY

Fruitquan Bailey
Da Boyz Of #C74: Rikers Island Legendz

This book is a work of nonfiction. However, to protect the privacy of individuals, some names, identifying details, and certain events have been changed or withheld. Any resemblance to actual persons, living or deceased, is purely coincidental and unintentional. The author respects the privacy and dignity of all individuals mentioned and has taken these measures to safeguard the innocent.

Published by Spines Publishing Platform
ISBN: 979-8-89569-430-5

Featuring: Big Belly Man Hec, Shoe Shine, Big Fruit, Black Mick, Saquan, Germ & Mitchy Love, Deluxe and more.......

March 1991: Fruit was in Midtown with Wise and Money Bag Sha trying to take some money digging pockets. Fruit found himself back in Midtown after taking that loss fucking with Nut out in Annapolis, MD which led to their bang out in the projects. Wise was back in Midtown after slipping and falling off to the point where he needed re-up money. And Money Bag Sha never left Midtown, not since he began digging pockets in the 80's! Money bag Sha was still trying to bounce back from taking his loss in LG, when the Gabbana Girls booked him for nearly 30K!

As they stalked 14th Street looking for a pocket, they ran into what Wise thought was it! Wise described the pocket as a Left, which were always hard to dig.

But Wise was good at what he use to do with Big Un back in the days, so he impulsed on the vic and dug his left pocket. Left pockets were always harder to dig because damn near everybody in Midtown was right-handed. Wise spanked the pocket, and as he headed down into the train station, Fruit and Money Bag Sha were on his heels.

Wise only ran down one flight of stairs before he stopped to turn around and show them the money! As Wise began to count the money at the bottom of the first flight of stairs.

An undercover detective came walking down the stairs, and as soon as he thought he was close enough to the three of them, the detective yelled "FREEZE."

Next thing you know, Wise tossed all the money in the detective's face, and the three of them took flight further down the stairs into the train station!

As they ran through the train station, they hopped the toll and kept it pushing down to the platform. Wise was leading the pack, and as they hit the platform; Wise kept it pushing with no regards! Fruit was running in the back, behind

Money Bag Sha! And Fruit knew exactly what was about to go down! Wise jumped off the platform and hit the tracks!

Money Bag Sha followed behind Wise and hit the tracks like it was nothing! Fruit on the other hand, had never hit the tracks before, and as he was running wild with these two, he hit the tracks, praying to God he did not slip and fall! The three of them ran on the tracks until Wise led them to an escape exit up out the ground on some real Ninja Turtle shit in the middle of a crowded Midtown Street! As they one by one crept up out the ground and tried to hit the nearest corner, police came out of nowhere and backed them down!

They got knocked in Midtown and the three of them were off to Rikers Island! Wise and Money Bag Sha were well seasoned with the Rikers Island trips.

Fruit would be making what will be considered his first rodeo, because his first trip to Rikers Island only lasted one night before he bailed out at the court building! Fruit was a little worried, but he knew his brother/comrade Butter was on in #C74 and once they got together it would be all good!

At least that's what he thought!

When Fruit hit #C74 he was sent to Mod #6 new jack house. And as he walked down into the Mod #6 tunnel, he wondered what was good with Butter, who was sitting down in #6 Lower Bing! All this shit was new to Fruit, and he was soaking it all in! After a day or two Fruit went to court, and as he sat in the receiving room bullpen, he heard someone call Butter's name.

There he was, Butter sliding through the receiving room on his way to get shackled and take his ride up north to serve his 22 To Life! Fruit was excited to see him.

They hadn't seen each other in almost a year, and a whole lot has occurred since then! Fruit called Butter by his name, and when Butter turned in his direction, Fruit noticed butter had a cut in his face! Fruit asked him what happened, and Butter briefly told him that it was a war going on that no man was safe from.

Some real Mobb Deep shit! Fruit tried to understand what he was told, and he geared up for his first rodeo! Fruit went to court and when he returned, he was moved to population Mod #9! And just his luck, he landed on the North Side (Brooklyn Side). When Fruit walked into the house, he spotted the dude Gary Ghee off N.A. Rock. Gary Ghee, Fruit and Butter had history!

The three of them went to JHS 117 together, and they hung out in the streets of Bedstuy, Brookly together as kids! Gary Ghee immediately put Fruit on point about the dude who cut Butter! And within a New York Minute, Fruit was on the nigga ass. Fruit and Gary Ghee put that work in for Butter as they stomped flames out the dude and stabbed him up with Bic Pens. But what Fruit didn't know was, he had just jumped himself into the Brooklyn v. Bronx Beef! Getting at the dude who cut Butter led to Fruit punching another Bronx nigga dead in his mouth in the #7, #8, #9 Building Tunnel coming back from the messhall. And that dude sending a crash dummy to try to cut Fruit behind the gate coming out the messhall the very next chow run. And all that shit went down during Fruit's first day in population in Mod #9. After the crash dummy tried to cut Fruit; they moved Fruit to Mod #8. Brooklyn was deep in Mod #8 South Side: Brownsville Mike, Dorian, Joe, Nitty and Dahu. They should have moved Fruit further away, because the very first chow run that put Mod #8 and Mod #9 in the corridor together, Fruit jumped off the line when he seen the dude that tried to cut him, and to his surprise, the whole Mod #8 North Side popped with him! Dudes were shaking out in the corridor for a nice little minute before the squad got shit under control.

Fruit got snatched up, and the crash dummy agreed it was Fruit who hit him! Fruit caught his first Infraction on Rikers Island and was waiting to go to the Bing! Not before he and the comrade Dorian out of Brownsville made a movie on the School Floor one day! Mod #9 North Side was still shaking out with Mod #9 South Side,

especially since Fruit got scratched. The comrades Damon from Sumner Projects and Popcorn out of Marcy popped on the dude Smoke from Brownsville, who was running hard with them Bronx boys in Mod #9 South Side. Damion and Popcorn poked the dude Smoke up in the #7, #8, #9 Tunnel coming back from the messhall. And after they hit him, the police moved him, and it wasn't far enough! They moved Smoke to #4 Upper, where he would attend the school building with Mod #8 and run into Fruit. Damon was the Comrade and he sent word to Fruit, to clean the nigga Smoke up. And as soon as Smoke landed on the school floor, Fruit ran him down, and put that work in. Dorian held Fruit down as Fruit poked the shit out of Smoke and got away!

Fruit had to sit down for 30 days on his first trip to the Bing!

He landed in #6 Lower Bing, next door to the comrade

Reese aka Moe from Brownsville! It's been a minute since they've seen each other!

They did a juvenile bid together in 89', and Moe pulled up on Fruit and the Young Guns one night in 90' as they jumped in Moe's whip six deep for Moe to drop them all off at Junior's Restaurant. Moe schooled Fruit to what was going on in #C74, who was who and what was what! After serving his 30 days, Fruit left Moe in the Bing and took his show on the road, down to #3 Lower aka The Terror Dome! #3 Lower had a reputation and the dudes that were in and out of #3 Lower in 90'/91' were considered some of the realest dudes in the building. For example, #3 Lower is the one spot where The Trilogy (Moe Dog, Dubo and Uny Un) were all housed at the same time.

And this was at the height of the Brooklyn v Bronz Beef! Uny Un got touched by a Bronx dude, and all hell broke out from there with The Trilogy, specifically The General Moe Dog!

The General was putting it on during the beef, and he wasn't playing with razors. Moe Dog was straight stabbing dudes in that beef!

Shit, one time he even whipped a muthafuka with a TV cord because the dude was bigger than him (Dog got at the dude because the dude and his man jumped on Little N.A. on the visit) and Moe Dog didn't have his knife! You better believe, Moe Dog whipped scrams ass with that TV cord! It was 91' summer in #3 Lower and the Brooklyn dudes down there were down there making it hot, for real! When Fruit rolled up in that spot, it was a crew of Brooklyn dudes all on one side, and the comrade Uptown from the Bronx /Harlem on the other side holding it down by himself! Uptown was the comrade from Juvenile History, and his Brooklyn Card was official!

The North side hitters were repping as well: Ant from Franklin Ave. was running two deep with the dude Vardo from Fort Greene, Don't Trust Just had the comrade Pito with him,Pretty Boy Star were on their LG shit,2 Deep, when Star came down from Up North for court!But Fruit clicked hard with the dude Poo Ching aka Inf from Fort Greene!

And it wasn't long before Maino pulled up, and Maino and Pretty Boy Star were acting a fool together in #3 Lower. There were several cuttings in #3 Lower that summer, you know you can't put a bunch of between Brooklyn and The Bronx! The bang out in the gym was pretty much a set up on behalf of them dirty ass police who wanted to see blood shed!

The Bronx house #2 Upper were already in the gym, as The Brooklyn House #3 Lower were in the yard. Somehow someway, the police shut down the yard and took #3 Lower to the gym. Once inside the gym, the two housing units went straight at each other! The comrade Toe Joe from Tompkins Project got cut that day, and all hell broke loose in that gym. After the gym incident, #3 Lower dude felt some type of way. They felt like the police lined them up, and it was time to bring the beef to a head! Fruit was working the midnight suicide in #3 Lower that summer, and he collected all the comrade's girlfriend's phone numbers and called all the chicks, to request visits on the A to Z visit the next day, so everyone could be on the visit at the same damn time! Of course, the chicks were down for the drama, so the next morning, the cells started popping for them visits! Brooklyn was deep as they traveled through the corridor with an escort to the visit!

The Bronx wasn't on point, and they weren't expecting Brooklyn to be deep on the A-to-Z visit! It didn't take long before Fruit fired the first shot! Shit hit the fan for real, and Fruit made it his business to get at the dude who cut one of the comrades / Big Homie "Don V" aka VJ off N.A Rock back in 90' when the beef was brewing!

Not that Don V needed anyone to do anything to revenge his cutting. VJ was cool as a cucumber about getting back at dudes, and that he did.

Don V made movies each time he popped out on niggas From closing the messhall gate as he cut whoever was in arms reach, to sneaking up in Mod #9 South Side and putting in that pain on the whole house! Don V was a problem! The Big Homie had muthafukas refusing to go on their visits because they didn't wanna get caught slipping by Don V! So, Fruit letting it go and touching something for Don V was nothing! In fact, Fruit touched two different dudes that day as razors and burners were being swung by everyone! Brooklyn was shaking it up: Fruit, Maino, Pretty Boy Star, Toe Joe from Tompkins, Hook Off and Big Head Wayne O from Grand Ave. And everyone put it down that day.

It was hectic, as Pretty Boy Star got scratched by the rude boy Shabba, and then Maino fucked around and cut Hook Off by mistake as they both jumped on a nigga at the same damn time, who had cut Hook Off previously, while they were in the Law Library. Yeah, niggas were getting cut anywhere and everywhere during that Brooklyn v Bronx Beef!

Yeah, the visiting room got shook up, as the adults, Big Rashawn and Mad Money Mark aka Uno, passed out burners in exchange for jewelry, arming up whoever! When the squad finally reported to the visit room, dudes were running around tossing razors and bangers everywhere. Big Rashawn and Mad Money Mark was mad as a muthafuka because they had to toss away Drugs, Razors and even some Jewelry. Yeah, Rashawn was not only working on the visit. The nigga was up there booking everything and everybody, if you couldn't hold it down!

Which led to an incident in #3 Lower that summer. The dude Rashawn booked a nigga name Dark Skin Troy from Queens.

Big Ra booked the nigga for a Diamond Flooded High Riser Ring, and the ring didn't belong to Troy. The ring belonged to the homie Kee Kee from Brooklyn, out of Roosevelt Projects!

When Big Ra booked the nigga, Troy gave that shit up with no hesitation. And when word got around the building, the homie Ant from Franklin Ave vowed to get at Troy if ever seen him because Kee Kee was Ant's homie! And out of nowhere, as the Brooklyn Squad was sitting in the #3 Lower Day Room, the dude Dark Skin Troy came down to #3 Lower!

When he pulled up, he peeped at how deep Brooklyn was on the North Side. So, he figured he'd go on the South Side with the homies Uptown from the Bronx/Harlem and Moe Joe from Harlem. Troy went on the South Side, and his very first day there, the squad ran down on Uptown.

The security team got word that Up was sitting on a New York Orange Box Cutter (that made that clicking sound as you extended the razor blade : old school shit) and they ran down on him, dragged him to the Bing and locked the house down! When they locked the house down, the C.O's then let Fruit and Inf aka Poo Ching, go on the South Side to sweep the floors after the squad violated everyone's cells during the cell searches. When Fruit and Inf rolled on the South Side, they noticed that the cells didn't have any gates on the doors. And just like the stick-up kid he was, Inf flagged Fruit's attention as Inf walked pass Troy's cell and seen Troy standing at his cell door with jewels swinging: Chain Hanging Low! And as Fruit caught on to what was going down, Fruit walked right up to Troy's cell door and yapped him for the jewels! Fruit and Inf then slid back on the North Side! When they got back on the North Side, only Vardo and Ant from Franklin Ave. were out their cells. And when Fruit showed Ant the jewels, Ant straight flipped! Ant began to scream about how he was gonna get at the nigga Troy, and Fruit cut his throat! That shit led to Fruit and Ant having to FIGHT! Fruit was totally offended.

Fruit lived by being : LOYAL TO A FAULT! And Ant's choice of words called Fruit a snake and or a backstabber! Fruit said fuck that, we gotta FIGHT! Ant and Fruit shook out in #3 Lower.

It was a fair one and a nice one at that! They shook hands after the fight, and Fruit put the jewels around his neck and kept it pushing.

As for Dark Skin Troy. He ain't want NO SMOKE, and him and Fruit didn't bump heads again until 2005, and at that time Big Fruit was one of the biggest niggas in the jail, lifting everything in the yard. It was best they both left that shit alone. Besides, Big Fruit was 3 years away from his Parole Board and he was trynna to get the fuck out of prison!

After the visiting room bang out, Fruit took another trip to the Bing. He landed in #1 Main Bing this time, with Lil N.A from N.A. Rock and Killa from Fort Greene. These two lil dudes had #C74 in an uproar during the Brooklyn v. Bronx Beef!

Fruit's stay in the Bing was short lived because he copped out to a bullet (One Year – 8 months City Time) for the Midtown case with Wise and Money Bag Sha.

Fruit took the rap and slid to #C76 after four months of banging in #C74! When Fruit went to #C76 he was on a different type of time! He approached the transfer on his bully for real.

Fruit told all the dudes in the bullpen, that when they got

to the #6 Building, he was gonna put it down and if muthafukas wanted to roll, they better had stepped up right then!

Fruit done experienced what this shit was all about in #C74. He watched the comrade Miz aka Quiet Mike from Bedstuy, take a whole phone in Mod #9, and there were some hitters in there. Ain't nobody say shit when Miz deaded that jack! Fruit also put his work in. He revenged Butter's cutting. He revenged VJ's cutting. And he ran wild in #3 Lower!

Therefore, it wasn't a question who the LIVEST NIGGA in that bullpen was! And that's the attitude Fruit took to #C76 and put the Adolescents in a choke hold. Fruit's four-month stint in #C76 was legendary. He had his little squad: Puerto from LG, Denbo from LG, Love from Midtown/Harlem, Puerto Rican Phil from Staten Island, Lil Inf from Bedstuy, Squeak from Fort Greene and Apple Head Shawn from N.A. Rock.

Fruit chased a crew of Harlem niggas up out of the South Mod once his man Dex aka Derrick from Queens went home.

Dex was the comrade from Juvenile History! In fact, Dex was the first-person Fruit made friends with in Spofford back in 87' when they were kids, the LOVE was real!

So, Fruit let Dex slide without getting caught up in his shit! Sending them Harlem niggas up out the dorm made Fruit HOT, and everybody was talking!

It was to the point where all the police were wanting to know who Fruit was! While the heat was on Fruit, you had dudes like Ralph Lo and Bad Vibes laying in the cut waiting to get back to the streets. Fruit slid through the #6 Building like it was nothing, and he was released on THANKSGIVING MORNING 91'.

Late 91' was hectic in LG! Fruit came home to World having the projects on SMASH! World was doing his numbers and mixing it up for real! Fruit had to find his way and do something. That Midtown shit was out the window. So, Fruit got with Puerto and they started hustling together. It was Fruit, Puerto, Peter Rab and Rayon. While World had the whole Young Gunz crew and then some.

It was all LOVE no matter what, because at the end of the day, they were all family. Puerto eventually got knocked off for a robbery he said he didn't pull off!

Fruit then got with Stack a Dollar and they hustled in LG as well as OT in Harrisburg, PA. It was a hell of ride for Fruit when he went home from the #6 Building.

The streets were moving fast, and before you knew it, Fruit was back on Rikers Island after seven months of freedom. This time he wouldn't be copping out to no City Time either. Fruit done came back to #C74 with a HOMOCIDE / MURDER Case, and everybody talking about it, because his victim was a female!

A very well-known female at that! Fruit got himself caught up in a scuffle with a group of chicks in LG, there was a struggle for the Desert Eagle .357 that Fruit possessed that night, and a shot went off! Fruit accidentally shot and killed one of the girls during that scuffle! He went on the run for a hot month or so out in Harrisburg, PA.

His days on the run were short lived as he got knocked in

Harrisburg, PA 92' summer, and made his way back to New York City in NYPD Custody!

It was 92' summer, and Fruit was being expedited from Harrisburg, Pa back to NYC on an outstanding warrant for MURDER! He was being accused of shooting and killing a 19-year-old girl back home in Lafayette Gardens Projects in Bedstuy, Brooklyn. The alleged crime of Murder back home in LG had the projects in an uproar. The projects dealt with tension like never before and the projects were divided as well.

The division came about because most people viewed the shooting was an accidental. The situation had Fruit so stressed out, he concluded that he'd try to cop out at his arraignment in Brooklyn Criminal Court, if he was charged with an accidental shooting! Not too advanced with the law and not knowing about any evidence or witness testimony against himself, Fruit didn't realize he was already indicted for MURDER, given his #INDICTMENT and there would be a TRIAL to get things resolved!

Once Fruit hit Rikers Island #C74 he already knew he had to get his ass in the Law Library. Word spread fast that Fruit was back in the building because he ran into Rod O off N.A Rock in the clinic. Although no pleasantries were exchanged, Fruit knew Rod O would spread the word, and that he did! Word got back to Ron K from Grand Ave. who was waiting to go up north on a 24-month violation, and Moe Dog who was now laid up in the building awaiting his bus ride up north as well. Dog had copped out to a 10 to 30 and his co-defendant Maino copped out to a 5 to 15 and they were headed up north any day. Moe Dog sent word for Fruit to meet him in the Law Library the next day. When they met up in the Law Library the next morning, Fruit told Dog exactly what happened. He showed Dog his #INDICTMENT and Dog began to read the fine print. Dog asked questions pertaining to the witness against him, and when we realized the witness testified at the GRAND JURY using a FAKE IDENTITY, Dog instructed him to pursue a perjury issue because Fruit's #Indictment was not a TRUE BILL! He informed Fruit that he needed to gather all his court documents as well as police documents to compare everything in its entirety. When they finished in the Law Library, they made their way to the corridor and were held up because Maino was being escorted in handcuffs to #1 Main Bing.

Maino was in the Bing for popping off on the police in the receiving room with the homie and comrade O.P from Flatbush Brooklyn!

Fruit got on his case as Dog instructed. Dog then went up north leaving Fruit to figure things out on his own! And that he did!

Fruit realised that not only did his witness testify under a false name at the Grand Jury, which is perjury, but it also means that his #INDICTMENT is not a TRUEBILL and the #INDICTMENT should be dismissed. Being young and ignorant of the law, Fruit never presented this issue the right way to his lawyer nor did his lawyer show any real interest. So, off and running Fruit went in #C74, just like hundreds of other adolescents that were in the same unknowing situation.

After one day in Mod #6 Fruit was ready for population.

He pressed the police in the bubble to be moved, and they quickly obliged him, sending him to Mod #8. When Fruit pulled up to Mod #8, the steady officer C.O Coy was working, and as he processed Fruit and sent him on the South Side, C.O. Coy thought Fruit looked familiar. As Fruit made his way to his bed, he recognized Hec, Kojack and Germ from the Bronx were in the house together. Familiar names and faces that Fruit would have to eventually get with and see what's good with those phones!

Before Fruit could put his bed together, C.O Coy called him back to bubble, and asked him to step out in the hallway! As Fruit walked towards the door, he noticed a perplexed look on Germ's face: Like what he wants with you, and why you going back out there! And like a dummy, Fruit walked out the door, was told by C.O Coy to put his hands and the wall and as soon as Fruit did what the officer told him to do, C.O Coy snuffed Fruit from behind, knocking Fruit dizzy! Fruit couldn't do nothing but grab his right eye and hope the muthafuka didn't keep swinging. C.O. Coy popped on Fruit because he remembered Fruit from 91' when Fruit jumped off the line in the corridor to get at a dude in Mod #9, and it led to a mini riot in the corridor. Fruit was in Mod #8 in 91' with a few Brooklyn dudes (Hec, Dahu, Dorian, Joe, Mike and Nitty) but he didn't stay there long.

Fruit was scratched in 91' when he was in Mod #9 during the Brooklyn v. Bronx beef. When Fruit got scratched, he was moved to Mod #8, where he ran wild for about a week (stabbing the dude who scratched him), and C.O. Coy remembered all that! Fruit was sent to the clinic, treated and had to wear an eye patch for a few weeks on his right eye.

Fruit was then sent to #4 Upper where the homie Black Mick from Brownsville was upstairs regulating on the North Side. When Fruit pulled up to the house Mick was excited to see him.

Fruit and Mick have a history from the mid 80's when Fruit used to visit his family in Howard Projects. Mick was a Golden Glove Kid back then and everybody knew it!

Mick was on Rikers Island for a MURDER CASE as well. Mick rolled out the red carpet for Fruit in #4Upper. Mick remembered his first day in #C74 and Fruit was the first person he'd seen coming out of the receiving room. Mick came through 91' summer, the same day Fruit and Brooklyn blew up the visiting room and had the building in an uproar.

Fruit called out to Mick, telling him to hold it down and not let anybody try to play him! Mick went on to the new jack house Mod #5, where he would be housed with a few other Brooklyn homies like Rumble and Diggy out of Fort Greene.. One dude Mick got cool with, and they both went to population together.

The other dude was a little more seasoned than Mick when it came to Rikers Island, and when they were in a population housing unit together, the dude tried to play Mick when it came to Mick's phone time! Mick wasn't no punk or no sucker. And he knew how to scrap. He was a Golden Glove Kid! Without hesitation, Mick put the beats on the kid! Putting lumps and bumps all over the dude head and face! And with Mick knowing he was in #C74 where dudes were playing razor tag and cutting each other for any and everything, Mick decided to blow the dude face off as well. Mick wasn't in the building 30 days before he found himself upstairs in #1 Upper (Admin-Seg) right on top of Fruit, who was downstairs in #1 Main Bing! Fruit and Mick would talk every day, about how it was going down in the building and how they weren't going to be playing games with dudes if they had to get it on. #C74 was crazy 91' summer, and Fruit eventually slid to #C76 to finish off his remaining 4 months on a city bid of 8 months! Mick went on to ride it out in #C74 and eventually landed in Mod #9 South Side which was a Bronx House. With the Brooklyn v. Bronx Beef pretty much dead, Mick and a few other Brooklyn dudes were posted up on that side and doing them! And one day while both sides were sharing a TV, the C.O.s chose to have 2 dudes fight for the TV, one dude from each side!

Over on the North Side there was the dude Sha Wells from Farrockaway, Queens. He was a cool dude, and he knew how to scrap. Sha Wells was seasoned at the Rikers Island thing, he'd been sliding through #C74 since 87' and he's always handled himself accordingly. On the Soth Side they had Black Mick from Brownsville! When these 2 dudes stepped out in the A/B gate they immediately began to shake out! Sha Wells was a little smaller and quicker than Mick, and he was fighting Mick using his 52 Hands Skills. Mick was a cruiser-weight waiting to smash something, as he went straight for the knockout as hit Sha Wells with some blows that shook the dorm walls and plastic windows! Mick wasn't taking the situation seriously, because he really didn't want to reveal his boxing skills. Sha Wells on the other hand, was going hard trying to secure that TV for the North Side. When it was all said and done, the C.O.s in the bubble awarded Sha Wells and the North Side the TV. The C.O.s were mad at Mick because they knew he held back. Mick wasn't about to become the dude who the police run to when they want to see dudes scrap! Mick said fuck them police and fuck that TV! Sha Wells then went on to become even more popular in #C74 because he had a fight with Black Mick.

Once Mick had enough with that fighting shit, he wasn't playing any games with dudes! Mod #9 South Side got into a beef with Mod #8, and they popped off in the corridor something crazy. And it was Mick in full action putting in that work.

Rumor has it, Mick may have poked up a C.O. that day in the corridor. When Mick found himself in #1 Main Bing early 92' he found himself rocking out with a dude name Kendeer out of Flatbush.

Kendeer was a comrade of Moe aka Reese from Brownsville. Keender was good people, and he wasn't no sucker. Kendeer had a beef with Deluxe from Tompkins Projects (who would eventually become one of DA Boys in 92'), and the dude Pito (The Comrade) from crown Heights popped with Deluxe. Deluxe was a straight shooter in the streets as well as in #C74. He made his bones in the building 90'/91'/9'2 and he was far from a sucker. Pito was the homie who'd been doing this with dudes since DFY, and he'd developed a rep known as The Herb Destroyer in #C74! Together, Deluxe and Pito took on Kendeer. So, Kendeer got with Mick, and together they got at Pito in #1 Main Bing.

Mick tried his hardest to dead arm Pito and knock him out, but Pito was on point. Kendeer tried his best to rag Pito, but he didn't get him as good as he wanted! Kendeer told Mick, he wanted to rag Pito worse than Shoe Shine did Hook Off back in 90'. When Pito escaped that situation, he and Mick began beefing. Mick was chasing Pito around #C74 but to no avail as Pito ran wild in #C74! Pito ran wild to the point where he was cutting so many dudes, he developed the nickname "Herb Destroyer" and rode it out until he slid up north on the same type of time! Pito went up north and immediately made his mark, chasing a nigga up into the C.O Bubble in Elmira Yard trying to cut the nigga.

Pito was WILDFOR THE NIGHT!

Kendeer eventually caught up with Deluxe and he caught Deluxe slipping, and Kendeer jumped out the #2 Building in #C74 and ragged Deluxe something serious. It was a cutting dudes remember. Deluxe was

also touched by the boy Alpo from Queens later that year in the meshall during the early morning Court Runs, and that cutting was memorable as well because Deluxe was supposed to go home that day with a NOT GUILTY VERDICT same as his codefendant Popcorn! Popcorn went home and Deluxe went to Kings County Hospital (KCH). Deluxe eventually came home within a matter of days. Keender would go on to do a light bid, only to return in the early 00's and ran into that damn Pito in Auburn Correctional Facility! And without question them two dudes got it shaking like it was 92' all over again! Only this time they looked like two grown ass men rolling over on the ground in the yard! They both had to laugh at that shit, and let the beef go after that last dance! Keender would eventually slide back to the streets of BK. Only this time he wouldn't be returning to prison, as he also loss his life when he was MURDERED in BK and found dead on the streets!

The summer was heating up and dudes in the Bing were getting riled up! There were a few homies in the Bing that Fruit hadn't seen since he was back in the building, and some of them were even beefing with each other! Early one morning the alarm went off crazy for an incident in#1 Main Bing, and the police in the building were petrified! Fruit was fresh back in the building, and to see the police so shook, he wondered who popped that morning! Then, the word got out through one of the C.O.'s (Poppa Smurf) that the homies Uptown from the Bronx/Harlem and OP from Flatbush, got it shaking on their way to the yard! O.P tried to touch Up, and the nigga Up loss his mind! They said the nigga Up tried to toss a muthafukn Walk Through Magnometer at the nigga O.P!

Uptown had the strength of ten men once O.P tried to touch him! That shit had the building buzzing for a minute, and security said Up had to go! Up took his show on the road to H.D.M Bing as he continued to do what he does, and that's be Up from Uptown! There was one memorable moment that took place with Up and the homie Dubo back in 90'.

The Brooklyn v Bronx Beef was cooking and the homie Uny Un of the Trilogy (Moe Dog, Dubo and Uny Un) got cut in the bull pen by a dude from the Bronx!

The situation led to an incident coming out the meshall, where Up and Dubo both got involved with the situation and they popped coming out the messhall. There was another little beef brewing between Up and Dubo that had the whole building buzzing! The chick who lined Pac up with the allegations that led to his conviction in New York, she tried to pull a move on the visit while visiting Dubo. The chick tried to pass her number off to Up, and all hell broke loose in that building!

With Up being the Comrade and Family, Moe Dog made sure, Up and Dubo worked that shit out. Up and Dubo were both Dog's brothers and Dog wouldn't have had it any other way!

The homie O.P would eventually slide up north and do something light before he returned to BK! Once he touched down, the homie slipped up during a Gun Heist with some undercover police and fucked around and got put down.

In fact, they say the homies Dorian and T-Roy from Brownsville, who would have been his codefendants, also got hit bad! The homie Dorian had on a Bulletproof Vest when it went down, and after the shots were blown, they say he was stretched out 10 feet away from his Vest as the pigs blew his Vest up off him! Good thing he was wearing that Vest!

Dorian and T-Roy would eventually get convicted and sentenced to stretches in the mountains. Dorian and T-Roy both would land in Clinton with Fruit in 95'. T-Roy and Fruit would run into each other first, and there weren't any pleasantries upon their introduction. Fruit aint know T-Roy from nowhere, and Fruit decided to full court press the nigga once he got wind about the SMOKE he was getting! T-Roy complied with Fruit, and then got on some funny shit once he got with Brownsville niggas in the jail. That shit had Fruit in a frenzy, which led to Fruit and T-Roy getting it to shaking on the Hill in Clinton, and the homie General from Brownsville would try come to T-Roy's aide, and Fruit shook out with both of them niggas on that Hill back in 95'. After serving a keeplock for that incident Fruit would run into Dorian, Drak and Black Reg both from East New York BK over in Clinton Annex!

The three of them dudes were in Clinton Annex laying low. Fruit pulled up and had to tell Dorian all about how he had to pop on the dude T-Roy! Fruit felt bad about the situation because as time was passing by, he was coming to find out that T-Roy was good people and he was a good dude! Dorian and Fruit had history from LG to #C74 so they didn't get into anything about that situation!

Meanwhile, the boy Mick had #4 Upper jumping. He had the C.O.s in the smash and the dudes in the house were playing their positions. Mick had 3 dudes who he introduced to Fruit. There was Ron Mack from the Bronx, Phil from Queens and Magoo from Queens. Ron Mack was a cool dude, and Mick really liked him. Phil was the coolest dude in the house. And Magoo was Mick son. Mick had Magoo making moves on that visit, bringing back that smoke. Then, Magoo came back with a nice size piece of jewelry around his neck. He made it back to the house safely because he was telling dudes it belonged to Mick. Sure enough, Mick got his hands on that immediately! As Mick ran around the building with one of the biggest chains, he also showed love as he let others borrow it.

One time Mick let his boy Rush out of Queens wear the chain. Rush had the chain for a few days, and Mick ended up going back to the Bing. Mick told Fruit to get the chain and keep it.

So, Fruit went in his cell, cranked open his window and called Rush out the window. Rush was in Mod #4 Lower at the time, and he responded accordingly, as he sent the chain up to #4 Upper with no problem. And this pretty much began the relationship of Fruit and Rush from Queens as they would eventually go off to serve some of their bids together in the late 90's.

Once Fruit got that first chain from Magoo, it was pretty much on! Word spread that Fruit was now yapping dudes for their jewels. It wasn't long before Big Belly Man Hec from Bushwick pulled up to #4 Upper. They were closing Mod #8 and Hec went up to #4 Upper North Side with Fruit. Hec and

Fruit knew of each other, but they never had any dealings whatsoever. But Hec was a real one, and when he pulled up to #4 Upper, he went straight to Fruit cell, sat on Fruit's bed and opened Fruit's locker. Hec let it be known that it was all love, and that they were there together 2 Deep! Hec was different. He was on his Rikers Island shit for real when it came to new niggas, herbs, lames and suckers.

Hec didn't like fronting ass niggas at all. His favorite saying was "That Nigga Pussy." And Hec would prove that so many dudes where in fact just that, pussy! Fruit and Hec clicked immediately, and together they smashed out #4 Upper like never before, as the beginning stages of Da Boyz began to come about!

While #4 Upper was ringing off, there was a cutting in Mod #8 that shook the building! The homie CB from Fort Greene got scratched in Mod #8 by another Fort Greene dude, and the building was buzzing. CB also landed in #4 Upper when he was moved up out of

Mod #8. CB landed on the South Side of #4 Upper, and he immediately put that side on smash and regulated the phone. Fruit and Hec tried to get CB to come on their side, but CB needed that jack! CB had a phone jones for real! While CB, Fruit and Hec were all upstairs in #4 Upper chilling, shots were being fired around the building for CB! One of the shots that caught Fruit's attention was a shot fired at his boy Sha from Fort Greene and Crown Heights. Apparently, Sha got caught up in that Fort Greene beef that left CB scratched. And when that happened, the General Moe Dog sent dudes at Sha! One of the dudes who touched Sha, would eventually land in #4 Upper with Da Boyz and Sha would handle his scandal! Sha was now laying low down in Mod #9 with a few of his

Fort Greene boys from the streets (Fly Ty, Lil Rob and Squeak). It wasn't long before Hec got trapped off for an old misbehavior report that would send him to the Bing. A few days before Hec left #4 Upper for the Bing, Little Head Moe Joe from Harlem pulled to #4 Upper North Side.

And when Hec bounced, it was Fruit & Moe Joe regulating #4 Upper. The infamous incident that sent Fruit and Moe Joe up out of #4 Upper, was when the dude Magoo walked over onto the South Side, and somebody cut the nigga! He came back on the North Side leaking, and he was acting as if he didn't want to get busy. Next thing you know, Fruit grabbed Magoo by his collar and dragged him back over on to the South Side, where Fruit made Magoo cut the nigga back. As Fruit and Magoo were trapped on the South Side, the boy Gerrod from Queens ran off the North Side up into the bubble, pushed the female C.O. out of his way and began pressing buttons and turning knobs to keep open the C Gate so Fruit and Magoo could get back on to the North Side safely. The female C.O. in the bubble pulled her pin and the squad came rushing up to #4 Upper.

When the smoke cleared, Magoo and the other dude both went to the clinic, and Fruit and Moe Joe got packed up to be moved up out of #4 Upper. They were first sent to #2 Main with Lil Ty from Kingston Ave and Twin from the Bronx. These dudes were on the burn in #2 Main with no phone or TV! Fruit and Moe Joe weren't staying there! They didn't even unpack their property as they told dudes in the house to fake a run out with them. Dudes agreed to help, and they began throwing garbage cans and mop ringers at Fruit and Moe Joe. The C.O.s in the bubble called the Captain and they moved them to Mod #4 Lower. Mod #4 Lower was a program house, and them shaky muthafukas did not want no parts of Fruit and Moe Joe. The housing unit refused them, and they were taken to the YM Pen where they slept for about 3 hours before being moved down to Mod #9.

Getting down to Mod #9 was the plan all along for these two! They were trying to get to a dorm instead of cells, and the North Side of Mod #9 was where all the homies were. They arrived at Mod #9 around 2 am, and the C.O.

working that night, sent them both on the South Side (The Bronx Side). Fruit and Moe Joe rolled up in the house and before they could get to their beds, they were approached by this big 6'6 Puerto Rican dude name Lou! Lou was a big dummy about to get his ass whipped! Lou told Fruit and Moe Joe that he had to search their property for drugs and weapons like he was the mutha-fukn police and or if they were bitch niggas! Before Lou could finish his sentences; Fruit punched him dead in his face and Moe Joe popped as well.

Before you knew it, Fruit and Moe Joe were whipping Lou ass in front of the bubble 2 o'clock in the morning. The C.O. in the bubble turned on the lights to see what was going on, and all he could say was "I never should have sent y'all over there." The C.O. calmed everything down without making any reports. Fruit and Moe Joe went on the North Side, and the beef with the South Side was officially on! When Fruit and

Moe Joe landed on the North Side of Mod #9 dudes were chilling and pretty much situated on that side. Whoever was claiming the phones at that time already knew what it was. Fruit didn't have to make a scene or give a speech. He told the dude in the last bed in the back of the dorm to pack his shit and move somewhere else. The dude did just that. Fruit slept in the very last bed in the dorm, right next to his boy Sha, who was laying low since the CB incident. Sha and Fruit were cool, and they had a familiarity through Fruit's family in Fort Greene. Moe Joe didn't last long in Mod #9, because he was determined to get at the dudes on the South Side for that stunt they pulled. Moe Joe got word that the dude Lil Bam from the Bronx was behind that shit, and Moe Joe was sending threats. One day when the South Side was out to commissary, the feed up arrived at the dorm. The police weren't on point as he allowed a few dudes from the North Side to prepare the feed up. As dudes were preparing the feed up, the Soth Side returned from commissary, and somebody clicked the doors open when the police weren't looking. All hell broke loose as dudes from the North Side ran out the dorm and popped on the South Side. The feed Up was all over the walls and floor, commissary bags were ripped, and commissary was smashed all over the place.

The police in the bubble pulled his pin and the squad came running. This incident made the dorm hot, and Moe Joe got picked off for being a19 year old adult and was moved out of the building.

Fruit and Moe Joe wouldn't see each other for another 7 years until 99' in Attica.

Fruit and Sha remained in Mod #9, and they regulated things together! Fruit had one phone and he gave Sha the second phone. Sha had his Fort Greene crew and Fruit had all the little stragglers from Brooklyn. Mod #9 North Side was the spot. Fruit had the dorm jumping. Everyone was getting along and there wasn't any in-house drama, other than trying to catch Lil Bam from the Bronx who was hiding out on the South Side. Everything was smooth until Moe Joe bounced, and Germ from the Bronx pulled up. Germ was the homie from them Mod #8 days, and he ran with Brooklyn dudes not only on Rikers Island, but Germ was heavy in the streets of BK at one time with several of the comrades! Once Germ pulled up, he and Fruit went on a mission. Germ and Fruit were hitting the corridors every day, 2- or 3-times a day, looking to book, rob and or yap some jewellery to exchange for Weed and Razors. One night Germ was on the jack talking to his girl a little too long for Fruit, so Fruit decided to snatch up Fly Ty and Lil Rob from Fort Greene to hit the corridor. The 3 of them walked to the Clinic area, and 2 adults were coming down the stairs from the visiting room area. As they walked past Fruit, Fruit didn't say a word to anyone about anything, he just yapped one of the adults for their jewellery and backed out his razor to make sure the adult nigga kept it pushing and respect the heist! When Fruit yapped the adult, Fly Ty and Lil Rob stood there emotionless.

They were shocked that Fruit did that. It was all fun and games until the very next day, when Fruit went to court. Fruit went to court with the new jewellery on his neck, and he ran into his homie and comrade Rayon from LG that was locked up in Brooklyn House. Rayon had on a nice piece of jewellery when they bumped heads, and Fruit somehow convinced him to switch jewellery with him! Fruit returned to Rikers Island with the new jewellery, only to find out that Mod #9 went to the Barbershop that day, and them adult niggas were looking for Fruit!

Germ thought it was so funny. And this is when Germ told Fruit how much he reminded him of Rondu from

Brownsville. Germ explained how tight the 2 of them were, and he mentioned how Rondu went at the adults about the same shit when an adult yapped Rondu in 90' and Rondu said "Can't No Adults Where Jewellery In #C74." Fruit then decided he wasn't going to hide from the adults. Fruit was able to get down to the Barbershop the next day, and when he went to the Barbershop, he had the jewellery on his neck.

Fruit went up in the Barbershop with 2 of the lil homies from Mod #9. He identified himself, letting them know who he be, and at that moment Fruit told them adult niggas "This Is My Muthafukn Building, Welcome To #C70 Fruit." And the legend began!... Fuit made it up out that Barbershop safely, and when he returned to Mod #9, he went straight to Sha and told him what happened. Sha was rolling with tears in his eyes as he started calling Fruit "Fruitzenegger!" But what goes around comes around! And that's exactly what happened to Fruit one day lingering in the corridor for dolo with no burner on him! Fruit slid up to the Medication Window to lurk in the corridor, and as the adults came out the messhall to line up on the wall, one of the adult niggas yapped Fruit! This shit had Fruit stunned! The first thing Fruit did was remember he didn't have a burner on him. So, Fruit took off his leather belt, wrapped it around his wrist, and begun chasing and whipping the adult nigga who yapped him! Fruit whipped the nigga so bad he dropped the jewels on his getaway!

RINGS
Black Mick
EVERLAST

Fruit went back to Mod #9 hysterically! Word got out that the adult nigga tried to yap Fruit, and the very next day a few adolescents popped on the adult nigga for Fruit in the Law Library!

Fruit went on to regulate Mod #9 North Side with all the lil homies out of Brooklyn that he had to make sure were always straight. Germ on the other hand, only had one lil homie in the dorm. Germ had his lil bro Pee Wee from Harlem with him, and we even called Pee Wee "Lil Germ" at one time. Pee Wee was smooth with it, straight Harlem nigga for real.

Pee Wee didn't too much talking, just a whole lot of listening and watching, because there was a whole lot to learn in this environment. Pee Wee went on to eventually utilize all his teachings, tutelage and survival skills to become one of the most respected members in the Blood Nation in the years to come.

As Big Fruit regulated Mod #9 North Side, there were a few comrades who came through Mod #9 and ended up landing on the South Side, only to have to shake out and get busy! There was the time when Lakey Da Kid out of Queensbridge came down there, and the South Side dudes tried to run him out of the house! Little did anyone know who the fuck Lakey was, and he showed muthafukas just who he be! When Lakey was shaking out on the South Side you could see him chasing dudes around the dorm. And when he got his hands on dudes, you could feel the windows shaking on the North Side! Lakey went all out, for real! And he never had that problem ever again. Then, there was the time when Shadow and Lil Chyna from Connecticut went over on the South Side! Shadow was fresh from Up North back on Rikers Island for another case. Chyna was new to Rikers Island and trying to find his way after dudes in #4 Upper South Side tried to rob him when he first pulled up.

Now they were together (Shadow and Chyna) on the South Side of Mod #9. Without question, Lil Bam from the Bronx sent dudes to Shadow and Chyna as soon as they got in the house. Of course, Shadow went crazy. He was not new to this, and he was gripped up.

Chyna rode shotgun with Shadow from that moment on for many years and plenty of cuttings and stabbings to come! Starting with Chyna trying to get at all of them dudes in #4 Upper on the South Side. Chyna made it out. He was cutting anyone and everyone he would remember from the time they tried to rob him. He accumulated a few slashings and Security put Chyna in Handcuffs as a Predicate Cutter. It was a while before Chyna would eventually catch the one dude he really wanted from that #4 Upper incident.

It was a little Puerto Rican dude out of Brownsville. Homie was supposed to be considered the homie out of Brownsville. He was chilling in #4 Upper on the strength of Mick because they came from the same hood. Plus, he was on the South Side with CB at one time, and he was CB

son! When CB went up north homie got beside himself in #4 Upper when him and another Puerto Rican dude tried Lil Chyna. One day coming back from court, the police in the receiving room slipped up and allowed Chyna to be strip frisked with the other inmates. Chyna should have been strip frisked alone as a predicate cutter. The police fucked around and strip frisked Chyna and the dude from #4 Upper together, and Chyna didn't give two fucks as he cut the shit out of homie right in front of the police as they both were being strip frisked. Chyna waited until they both were stripped down to their boxer shorts, and when the time was right, he gave homie the business. The police whipped Chyna ass that day. He didn't give a fuck. He came back to #1 Main Bing happier than a muthafuka after finally catching that dude who pushed that button on him up in #4 Upper when he first came through!

Shadow went on to do damn near the same things as he ran around the building hunting for the dudes from Mod #9 South Side. Shadow and Chyna took that shit personally and Lil Bam was who they really wanted.

Shadow and Chyna both landed in #1 Main Bing as predicate cutters for months to come before leaving #C74. Mod #9 North Side wasn't always crazy! They had some good times in the back of the dorm on Saturday nights as they would spray baby powder on the floor and slide around in their Fila slippers as if they were on roller skates, listening to their headphones with Bentley's LIVE Saturday Night rocking on the radio. Fly Ty from Fort Greene would lead the crew with this idea as well as with his very own dance. Fly Ty was smooth like that.

Then, there were the times that brung dudes together and opened dude's eyes to what camaraderie and family really meant. Tere was the time when Fruit and lil Dante from Fort Greene were in #1 Main Bing, and Dante was called to the Chaplain's Office. At the same time, Squeak and Fly Ty were both in Mod #9 together as they were both called to the Chaplain's office as well.

It was a sad day when Squeak loss his dad and they loss their uncle! They were all biologically related, and they were all considered family to the homies in the building.

This was a moment when everyone sat back silent, doing their own soul searching as they reflected on their lives as they were all approaching adulthood while incarcerated facing long term sentences. Squeak, Fly Ty and Dante all stood strong as they all made their way up north. Squeak and Fly Ty did short term sentences, while Dante was serving 15 to Life and accumulated more time as the years went by. Dante was the youngest of the family, and he was by far the illest! Dante came through #C74 like a hurricane in 93' as he made a name for himself from the gate! When he went up north to Comstock : Gladiator School, he didn't waste any time popping and catching a new bid. He and the boy Chyna from Connecticut were thick as thieves as they ran wild in Comstock together. Both ended up serving extensive stays in and out of the Box up north, as their names rung out in population like 6 O'clock!

Big Belly Man Hec made a stop in Mod #9 North Side! And when Hec pulled up, he and Fruit were inseparable! It was like they were back in #4 Upper together. Only this time, Hec and Fruit both had their own little crews within the dorm!

Hec was on his Bushwick shit, so he had his boys Rome and Perfecto running with him. Fruit had his little man Weez from Bedstuy and another littler dude name Homo who was claiming to have a baby by Fruit little cousin in the street. It was all love. Sha had the Fort Greene crew chilling, and Germ had himself, Pee Wee and tall Pop both from Harlem!

It didn't take long before Hec would wild on something or someone and eventually get moved out of the dorm. And it went down the day Hec wild out on Homo! Something happened between Fruit and Perfecto days prior, when Fruit wild on Perfecto for talking reckless about that jack. Fruit smacked the dude around a little something. Nothing major because he was Hec's little man. Hec was tight! He told Fruit he owed him one. And then, Homo played himself! Whatever Homo said or did, it led to Hec straight wilding on him! Hec grabbed ahold of him and got to beating on him as he grabbed him by his throat and banged his head on the bubble window a few times before he tossed the nigga on the floor and smashed him in his head with 2 plastic chairs. Hec wild out for real. In fact, defined the terms Wild Out and Wild On Something! Hec would go overtime on a nigga and the police in the building knew it!

Which is exactly why they sent Hec back up to #4 Upper after that ass whipping, he put on Homo. All Fruit could do was laugh, because Hec forewarned him, that he was going to get Fruit back, and that he did! Mod

#9 was cool for Fruit & Hec, because they had the chance to sleep next to each other in the back of the dorm, and they stayed up late nights kicking it on a personal level. That's when Hec told Fruit about his kids! Hec was the proud father

of Twins: Shameek & Shamel. Hec loved his kids, and whenever he was on the jack with his kids, he always seemed at peace! And you'd never hear Hec speaking Spanish, unless he was on the jack with his kids!

While Fruit & Hec were in Mod #9 together, Hec would always tell Fruit there was a dude on the South Side who would receive packages with Ounces of Weed in them! The Dude name was Cock Eye from the Bronx, and Lil Bam had him under the wing on the South Side, as them dudes smoked lovely! The dudes on the North Side were Thugging & Bugging!Hec wanted to get his hands on Cock Eye so bad. Until one day, Hec and Fruit were running the hallways, and they ran into Cock Eye as he was at the Package Room Window. Hec peeped it immediately, as he told Fruit "That's It."

Cock Eye was on point as he peeped the two of them creeping up behind him. Cock eye tried to pull a move and stop at the Captains Office, but Hec and Fruit dipped in the #2 Building, and laid low on him! When Cock Eye came strolling down the corridor, Hec and Fruit jumped out the #2 Building and snatched Cock Eye back into the #2 Building stairway!

When they snatched him up, Hec snatched the package and passed it to Fruit as Hec backed Cock Eye down with the Gem Star! Fruit opened the package, and there were a pair of sneakers inside. Hec told Fruit to tear out the soles inside the sneakers, and when he did so: JACKPOT... The dude Cock Eye had the motherload stashed inside the sneakers. Fruit tore out one big bag of Weed and one small bag of Cocaine! They were about to party like a muthafuka on the South Side of Mod #9, but Fruit and Hec interrupted all of that! And when they booked the nigga Cock Eye from the Bronx, all he asked for was a little bit of weed to take back to Lil Bam. Hec looked at the nigga like he was crazy when he asked that shit. And in true Big Belly Man fashion, Hec sprinkled the nigga a Blunt and told the nigga to kick rocks!

Rikers Island

It was the end of 92' and as the Christmas Holiday rolled around, the homies out of RedHook Projects came through! They will forever be known as "The Red Hook Three" due to their reckless shooting in Redhook Projects where they were firing at each other and they unintentionally shot and killed their neighborhood's school Principal : Mr P. Daly of P.S.15. When the three of them came through (Shamel, Kay and Russ) it was a circus in NYC as well as the #4 Building! Shamel came through first, and he went straight to #2 Lower Administrative Segregation where their were a couple steppers doing their thing!

That shit aing't mean a muthafukn thing to Fruit as he made his way down to #@ Lower with the homie Ron Mack riding shotgun. Fruit rolled up in the A & B Gate of #2 Lower North side, and there Shamel sat in the dayroom nervous as fuck but playing it cool. And when Shamel seen Fruit, he was relieved. Then, Fruit went straight "Fruitzenegger" and damn near threatened the whole Cell Block including the police! Fruit told them muthafukas, if Shamel get a fucking paper cut down there in that house, It's Lit! Shamel was happy as fuck, but nervous now!

Rikers Island

Fruit put a spotlight on his homie and Shamel knew he would have to hold it down! Shamel was in the building for maybe 2 days! Next thing you know, Shamel was transferred to Brooklyn House (as an Adolescent) which was unheard of! He was moved so the other two codefendants could be housed in #C74 together. They had a major separation between these dudes because of the RedHook Shooting! And as Kay & Russ settled in the building, they was good! Weird shit is, they were in #C74 for no more than 6 months for their High Profile Case, and they went to Trial, Got Convicted and went up north to serve 25 To Life, all in 6 months top!.. Unbelievable! They weren't playing no games with them boys who were apprehended for killing that Principal!

At one time, Sha aka Sayquan came up to #4 Upper!

When Sha came up to #4 Upper, Da Boyz were deep! Fruit, Hec, Mitchy Love, Deluxe, Steve O and Sha were all in one house! Then, one day the dude L' who touched Sha a few months back landed on the South Side of #$ upper. And it wouldn't be long before Da Boyz made Sha handle that! Sure enough, one day a female CO left the C Gates open, and Steve O strolled on to the South Side. He came back immediately, to let Sha know the gate was open, and the dude L' was sitting on a crate using the phone! Sha was a little nervous, but he stepped to his business as he creeped and crawled through the Gate over to the South Side and jumped dead on L' ass! Sha touched the nigga back, then slid back on the North Side!

When his nervous ass slid back on the North Side he stood up too soon, and the female CO in the bubble peeped him! She pulled her pin and the squad came running up to #4 Upper! The female CO tried to get us all to lock in, but we refused! And when the squad pulled up, it was a standoff in the dayroom, between Da Boyz and the Riot Squad.

Pee Wee
Mitchy Love
Bam
Germ

Harlem / Bronx

POLO
Pee Wee

Uptown
Maino

Da Boyz refused to lock in, and they told the police they weren't taking Sha anywhere! Da Boyz let it be known the C.Os in the #4 Building, knew L' cut Sha and now Sha got his ass back!

To everyone's surprise, the squad left the situation alone, as L' went to the clinic and Da Boyz kept regulating the building!

When Hec and Mick were regulating #4 Upper, they weren't leaving no rocks unturned, and dudes had to produce if they wanted to live in #4 Upper. There was one time a dude was supposed to go down on a visit and bring back some smoke for Hec and Mick! The dude went on the visit and swallowed a few balloons. When he got back to the house, Hec and Mick were ready to smoke! And when the dude told them, he swallowed the balloons, they were tight! Mick made the dude drink shampoo to vomit and through up those balloons. When that didn't work, Hec and Mick took the dude in his cell, and turned the dude upside down, as if to shake the balloons out the dude stomach, up out his throat! These two dudes were SAVAGES in #4 Upper! One time a dude came off the visit with the smoke, and when Hec took the dude in the cell for the dude to get the balloons out, as they were in the open cell, the ERU search team rolled up in the house! Everyone was surprised and off point when they bust through the door. Hec was on point tho! The dude had the balloons out with a little bit of feces on the balloons when the ERU burst in the joint!

Hec, grabbed the dude by his throat, and shoved the balloons down the dude's throat, to avoid getting knocked or taking a loss. Hec had to smoke! Then, it came a time when Hec and Mick both, had to dumb out on something in a major way. Hec had the infamous Crate Gate incident when he beat blood out a dude with a plastic crate.

The dude was getting to lose with it in #4 Upper! The dude was also one of them big dumb niggas who'd do anything to be down! So, when Hec had a run in with the dude, Hec ain't play with that nigga. Hec beat the niagga upside his head with the crate from the Bubble, inside the Day Room and back out the Day Room, in front of the Bubble!

The big silly muthafuka stood in front of the Bubble crying like a little chick! Mick was smashing shit up as well. He knocked one dude out so bad on the South Side of #4 Upper fucking with CB.

Everybody knew CB was a funny muthafuka, and one day he set a nigga up for failure when he told the nigga to hook off on Mick! The dude a big silly muthafuka who ain't know no better!

So, the nigga tried to hook off on Mick, and Mick hit the nigga with a quick 3 piece that bslumped the nigga straight to sleep! After that, dudes knew to beef with Mick from a distance, because if he get up on you, it's NIGHT NIGHT! There was the incident with Ring Dog out of Albany projects, where Mick could not get the nigga the way he wanted!

Which led to Shoe Shine not liking Ring Dog at all. They were Da Boyz and Shoe ain't fuck with Ring Dog at all. Fruit never really got up on Ring Dog either. Fruit was in handcuffs most of Ring Dogs time in #C74 with Fruit. Then Fruit turned adult, got up out those handcuffs and was moving around #C73 with Wise. One day Fruit went to court and when he peeked into the adolescent pen, Ring Dog was standing in the middle of the bullpen, and he was wearing a Sky Blue/Yellow and White Pelle Pelle! A leather jacket that Fruit done seen before, back home in LG! Fruit pressed Ring Dog and told him to come up out of World's leather jacket! Ring Dog tried to resist at first. He said World left it to him when World went home.

Fruit wasn't trying to hear that! Fruit told that nigga straight up "Come up out that leather before I asked the police to let me in the fucking bullpen." Ring Dog came up out that leather jacket, slid it through the bars to Fruit, and Fruit rolled out! When Fruit got back to #C74 and walked in the hose with the jacket on, Wise was bugging the fuck out! How you get that? Is what Wise asked him! All Fruit could do was laugh!

The relationship Hec and Fruit shared was special in it's own way! They were brothers and comrades, no longer just friends or homies! This bond was different! And when Hec went back up to #4 Upper North Side he was now with Mick!

These 2 here were on a different type of time up in #4 Upper. They were straight manhandling everyone and anyone who came through that door that wasn't people and or family!

It was rumors of the two running down on dudes for EVERYTHING! If word got back to them that a dude in #4 Upper (Either Side) and or #4 Main (Both Sides) had razors and or weed,

Hec and Mick were on their ass. Dudes were setting it out! Mick wasn't playing any games at all! And as they did their thing in #4 Upper, they had their little crew as well as some stragglers. The boy Rod O off N.A Rock was a straggler at the time, and Mick and Hec were treating him just like that, a straggler. Giving him the roach clips after their smoking sessions. Rod O was a funny dude, and for some reason he wouldn't go live downstairs in #4 Main with the other N.A. Rock boys (Leon, Lil Bucky) who were down there with Shoe Shine and Black Kasseem chilling with their feet kicked up.

Instead, he lingered in #4 Upper until the day he pulled a Suicide stunt to get moved out the house.

All he did was make #4 Upper hot, and when security rolled up in the house, they realized Mick was 19 years old and he had to go! So, off went Mick to the adults, up out of #C74!

And Mick left word that Rod O was food and for someone to get at that nigga for that bullshit he pulled! Hec was on deck when it all went down, and he was furious with Rod O.

Fruit at the time was in Mod #9 totally oblivious to anything that may have occurred up in #4 Upper. Rod O stunt got him moved to #2 Upper. And at that time there really wasn't anyone up there. Lakey Da Kid was on one side with his feet kicked up. So, Rod O went on the opposite side where there wasn't anyone to prevent him from

locking down the house.

Early one morning Fruit pressed the police for a Sick Call Pass because he got word that High School Students were walking the corridors. And when Fruit hit the corridors from Mod #9, and he ran into Rod O. Together they walked down to the receiving room to see if they could get a peek at the High School students touring the building. On their way back from the receiving room, they ran into Hec, Sha, Mitchy Love and the nigga Steve O! Mitchy Love was Germ's co-defendant. A smooth, quiet Puerto Rican dude. Steve O was supposed to be the homie, but certain dudes didn't fuck with him because they say Steve O told on the boy Scar when he cut the shit out of Steve O in 91'. And Steve O would eventually go on to snitch and testify against his co-defendant in a Murder Trial. Steve

O and Rod O also had history, as Steve O once tried to cut Rod O in #1 Main Bing Yard. And when they all ran into each other that day, Hec let it be known that Rod O was food and that if Mick was there, it would be go time! They all walked back down the corridor toward the housing units. When they got to the #2 Building, Rod tried to slide upstairs and Fruit fiend him out. At least he tried to do so. Rod O was fighting for dear life as he dragged Fruit on his back, up the stairs to #2 Upper. As Fruit was choking this nigga out, Hec and Sha were stripping the nigga of his rings and things while Mitchy Love played looked out! Hec and Sha were in and out on the robbery! And at the last moment, the nigga Steve O tried to get in the mix to cut Rod O. As Rod O dragged Fruit on his back up to #2 Upper, Rod O made it to the damn door and knocked on the window.

The door clicked open, and a female officer came running out to help Rod O; Fruit had to put her on her back pocket! And when Fruit released Rod O from the choke hold, Rod O popped on the nigga Steve O! It was a known fact that the nigga Steve O couldn't fight, so Fruit had to double back and help the nigga Steve O, and when Fruit and Steve O tried to get away, they ran into the ERU Search Squad, who had Hec, Sha and Mitchy Love all on the wall waiting for add Fruit and Steve O to the equation! The ERU Seach Squad dragged Da Boyz to the receiving room YM Pens where they all sat for about 3 hours until the shift changed at 3pm. Later, that evening Da Boyz all met up in the corridor again, to go up to #2 Upper and press the nigga Rod O because they knew Misbehavior Reports were coming and they were trying to avoid Bing Court and or Bing Time! When they were in the #2 Upper A&B Gate talking to the nigga Rod O, all he wanted were the rings to be returned. Fruit told Rod O "We Don't give Nothing Back After a Robbery" and Rod O said, "Fuck It Then, Ya'll Niggas Going to The Bing."

Everyone was looking at the nigga like he was crazy. And that's when Big Belly Man Hec said, "All y'all muthafukas up here on this side of #2 Upper, got beef." And the beef was on for real!

Da Boyz from #4 Upper were so furious with the nigga Rod O, they began to dumb out on everybody!

Early mornings in the #4 Building were always full of action. And when Fruit and Deluxe ran into the dude Sha Wells from Farrockaway, Queens one morning. Sha Wells was laying low by the Barbershop when he flagged Fruit down.

He let Fruit know some dude was in the Barbershop and he was waiting to book the nigga. Fruit said, "Fuck It" and rode shotgun with him! When the dude came out the Barbershop, Sha Wells stepped straight to his business and yapped the dude for his shine. Fruit then straight dead armed the nigga! As Fruit and Sha Wells tried to breeze, the dude began to chase behind them screaming and yelling that "They Took My Daughter Chain." It was straight comedy as they got away by dipping in the Law Library. The Law Library was a hot spot.

Because the very next morning, Da Boyz shut the Law Library down when Deluxe yapped the dude Cock Eye from Queens! Deluxe had a nice piece of Herc around his neck, that he booked a nigga for at court! Deluxe needed a nice size medallion for his chain, and Cock Eye had the piece he needed! It was already bad blood between them, because Deluxe ain't like the nigga.

He ain't like the nigga because Deluxe old codefendant Popcorn from Marcy, had blew the shit out of Cock Eye in Mod #9 a year prior! Popcorn cut Cock Eye real bad in his face while the nigga Cock Eye was sleep in his bed! NASTY WORK! So, Deluxe yapped the nigga in the Law Library, and all hell broke lose when Cock Eye tried to get busy. Shoe Shine was the first to pop after Deluxe yapped the nigga! Next thing you know, Hec tried to bust the nigga in the head with a chair. Fruit didn't pop! He was too busy trying to resolve another issue that was going down in the Law Library between Squeak and Man, both from Fort Greene. The two of them had a beef from the streets, and shit was about to get crazy!

The Law Library was crazy that morning, especially with dudes getting at Cock Eye and the police couldn't do shit! It was on them dudes that day to spare that nigga Cock Eye!

They left the nigga alone, as Deluxe slid up out the Law

Library with the jewels. And the police didn't flag nobody for the incident, as Da Boyz walked up out of that muthafuka like they owned the jail!

As Da Boyz waited to see what was gonna happen at Bing Court fucking with Rod O silly ass, Hec and Fruit kept rolling! And one day Hec was leading the charge through the corridors, and he peeped some nice big shit on a Puerto Rican adult nigga neck! Hec flagged Fruit's attention and began to follow the adult. What Hec didn't know was, the Puerto Rican dude was on point, but he was only focused on Fruit! When the adult Puerto Rican dude peeped the move, he put his back on the wall and called Fruit out! Hec was trying his hardest to get up on the nigga, but the spot was blown! The adult Puerto Rican dude turned out to be a major player with the Latin Kings, and he put word out that the beef was on with Fruit! Hec kept Fruit in some shit!

Then the very next day, Fruit went on a visit and got stuck in the count! As Fruit waited to leave the visit, the adult Puerto Rican dude from the day before, popped up out of nowhere, and he had about 2 or 3 dudes with him! Fruit was assed out! When the count cleared, Fruit tried to high step up out of there, but the Puerto Rican dudes followed him.

They played themselves by not popping on the spot. Fruit was ghost! And when Fruit hit the corridor, they kept following him, until Da Boyz popped up out of nowhere!

Fruit's prayers were answered when Hec and Shoe Shine came strolling down that corridor on their way to Sick Call and the visit! Next thing you know, Da Boyz and the Latin Kings were shaking out in the corridor, blowing the roof of the #4 Building, between the visiting room stairway and the Control Bubble! The squad came running out that Control Bubble so muthafukn fast it was crazy! The adults were dragged to the receiving room and shot up out of the building, as Da Boyz sat in the YM Pen for a few hours, with Shoe Shine still receiving his visit: Shoe Shine weight was up in that #4 Building! The incident was a movie for real, and Fruit name was stamped on a beef with the Latin Kings for years to come.

Fruit and Steve O eventually went to #1 Main Bing to serve 30 Days for the Rod O heist. Rod O did some suker shit and refused to testify at their Bing Hearings. As Fruit and Steve O sat in #1 Main Bing locking directly across from each other, they began to bond a little more! Fruit even hooked him up with a chick. One day Steve O came back from court and said he was gonnna start his trial soon.

And when his trial began, he was on trial for only one day, before returning to Rikers Island and telling Fruit, he copped out in the middle of his trial, taking a 5 to 15.

Fruit was envious for real. He told Steve O he was good with that bid. Fruit hadn't been offered a cop out on his case simply because the DA wanted a Murder conviction.

Fruit would eventually beg forced to trial, because he never received an offer! Steve O on the other hand, was pulling a move (Ratting On His Co Defendant) to receive his offer, and the truth wouldn't be exposed to Fruit until 95' when Fruit ran in to Steve O's Co Defendant who had all of his Trial Transcripts (Steve O's Testimony). Steve O would get out the Bing before Fruit, and when he did, he returned to population to find out that the homie Mack Murder was in the building fresh from Spofford with new assault charges.

Fruit
Bam

Deluxe
liberty

9
Butter

Don V aka VJ

Dubo

Mack Murder was the homie from Bushwick who everyone knew from Spofford, where he had been bidding since 90' for a Triple Murder he was convicted of as a 14 year old kid.

Mack was now on #C74 and he was lit from the moment he stepped through the door! Steve O must have thought something was sweet about Mack, because Steve O tried to yap Mack.

The nigga Mack went down on his first visit and came back with the biggest jewels in the building, and when Steve O ran into Mack one early morning in the meshall waiting for court, he tried Mack! Steve O fucked around and got yapped himself, as Mack yapped him right back on the spot, then commenced to beating the shit out of Steve O. It was apparent that the nigga Steve O couldn't fight, and every time he was forced to scrap, he got his ass whipped!

#1 Main Bing was in an uproar at that time. All the wild adolescents were in #1 Main Bing, and the South Side was HOT! Fruit, Shadow, Chyna, Tank Head Shawn, World, Puerto Rican Phil and a whole lot of other dudes!

One evening dudes in the Bing were bored to death, and they decided to get on their gates and make a whole lot of noise. And kit didn't take long for #1 Main Bing to respond!

The police cracked all the cells on the South Side and told everyone to step in the dayroom. When everyone was in the dayroom, they had all the adolescents stand in a big circle with two CO's standing in the middle of the circle, giving a speech! They all stood there and listened to the police threaten them with acts of violence if dudes don't stop making noise and or creating problems for the CO's while they were in the bubble chilling! Basically, the police were trying to silence niggas so they could kick back and have to do no real work throughout their work shift! It was totally understandable, but the threats of violence didn't sit well with Fruit! And in true Big Fruit fashion, Fruit spoke up right then and there, as he told the CO's and the adolescents, he wasn't going to be nobody punching bag, not while he is sitting in jail for MURDER. Kojack was laughing like a mutha-fuka when Fruit stepped up. He told Fruit to be careful, but Fruit ignored Kojack and spoke his mind right then. Fruit told all the adolescents that they were all about to take some long rides up north, and conflict with the police gonna be real. So, it starts here on Rikers Island for Fruit, and he refused to allow the police in #1 Main Bing to handle him and or put their hands on him. Fruit told the adolescents "I was throwing shots and ducking bullets in the street, and I'm not here to be NOBODY'S PUNCHING BAG!"

Fruit set the tone that evening in #1 Main Bing and the police recognized Fruit was gonna be a problem from that point on! There was one C.O in #1 Main Bing who kept it real with Fruit! C.O. Pickering aka Big Pic!

C.O Pick rolled up to Fruit cell one day, and asked Fruit if he knew the dude Kwan from Brevoort Projects in BK? Fruit knew exactly who he was referring to.

The dude Kwan use to roll through LG with Big Nut! Never did Kwan and Fruit have any issues. Well, Kwan must have thought different, because the nigga Kwan checked in PC using Fruit name, and C.O. Pickering didn't respect that shit! Which led to C.O. Pickering acknowledging Big Fruit and giving him his Lock Out Props in #1 Main Bing! Meanwhile back in population, Big Belly Man Hec and the #4 Upper North Side were picking dudes off from #2 Upper. They were running down on everything coming up out of #2 Upper South Side!

Rod O silly ass put all of them dudes in the line of fire for real. And then on one spring day, security in #C74 called themselves opening the Big Yard for the adolescents!

Mannnnnn, why they do that! That shit lasted 2 days tops! The first day was a MOVIE! They ran the houses out to #2 Upper yard, and as some of the houses waited for other houses to come out, the silly ass dude Rod O strolled out to the yard. He was a character for real! He slid out there on his smooth shit and he even had a few crash dummies with him! Big Belly Man Hec was thirsty for the blood of Rod O, so Hec went straight to the main gate and when they opened that gate, Hec slid straight to the back of the Big Yard and sat on the bleachers. Of course, the whole #4 Upper North Side was on deck! And when Rod O came towards them bleachers, Hec step straight to his business! Hec was on Rod O ass. To everyone's surprise Rod O didn't back down. He was nervous as hell. But he didn't back down!

Hec didn't tear the nigga head off, because they both were swinging Rug Cutters. Neither one got cut, nor knocked off! In fact, they both left that yard with big rips and tears in their hoodies and leather jackets! The #4 Upper Boyz went crazy that day. That was the day them dudes had the opportunity to show Hec they get busy!

As for the second day they opened that Big Yard. It was the Legendary Shoe Shine who shut shit down for real, for real. By this time Shoe Shine had taken a liking to World and

Chyna, who were both in #1 Main Bing. And once Chyna finally cut the nigga from#4 Upper South Side who tried him, Shoe Said fuck it, I'll be sure to clap the 2nd muthafuka who also tried that bullshit on Chyna. And in Shoe Shine fashion, he caught the dude on the steps of the #2 Building during the Big Yard run, and Shoe gave him the business. Shoe tour the nigga face off, and that was the end of Shoe Shine in#C74 Adolescents. Shoe got knocked off and ended up in #6 Lower Bing with Fruit (Fruit was moved from #1 Main to #6 Lower). Fruit and Shoe rocked out for about a week, they snatched Shoe, and pushed him to HDM Bing as an Adult. Shoe Shine and Lakey Da Kid would both take that ride together. Not only were they both considered adults now, but they both had the worst cuttings in the building at that moment, with Lake fighting a new charge for his cutting. Them niggas had to go!

When Da Boyz blew up the Big Yard, Fruit was still in the Bing, and he wouldn't be getting out any time soon. Fruit fucked around and went to the #1 Main yard one morning with at least 15 other dudes in the Bing. It was a nice spring morning, so dudes were outside in the Bing! Fruit happened to be screaming upstairs in the window to #1 Upper because there were a few adults up there he knew.

And as Fruit was holding a conversation with Micah from Bedford Ave./LG, a fight broke out and someone got cut. The police pulled the pin, and the squad came running!

Everybody in the yard spread out and got on the wall for the squad! And when the Chinese Captain (Cpt. Sang) reported to the incident, he stepped straight to Fruit!

Fruit tried to explain that he didn't have anything to do with the incident. And the Captain straight slapped the shit out of Fruit! He slapped the shit out of Fruit in front of all his peers and the adults up in the window! Next thing you know, the dude Born Son out of Brownsville yelled out the window to Fruit "You better put that work in" and that's exactly what Fruit did! Fruit blacked out as grabbed a whole of the Captain and tossed him around like a rag doll. Fruit slammed the dude on his head in front of his fellow officers and ain't nobody move! Everyone was shocked! Next thing you know, all the dudes in the yard came up off the wall and started fighting with the other officers, as the adolescents scream "REVOLU-

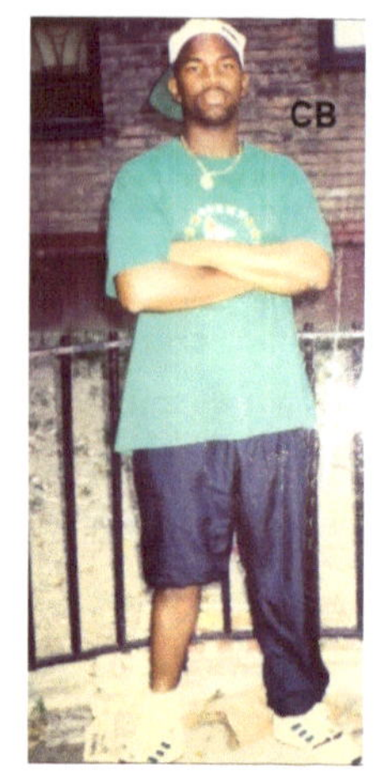

TION." It was some funny shit, yet it was real! Fruit avoided an ass whipping in a major way after his brutal assault on the Captain. When Fruit was done with the Captain, he refused to be handcuffed unless it was CO Ebron from #1 Lower who would cuff him and escort him to the YM Pen! C.O. Ebron cuffed Fruit and escorted him to the receiving room with no further incident.

C.O. Ebron had a talk with Fruit and let him know he would be ok and that C.O. Ebron would make sure none of the other officers tried no get back shit. He also told Fruit "You Never Let Another Man Slap You In Your Face" as if Fruit didn't already know that shit! The other officers were furious because Fruit got away with that shit. Next thing you know, Fruit was changed into a Grey Jumpsuit, took 6 Receiving Room Security Photos and was placed in Handcuffs permanently from there on in #C74!

Fruit walking around in Handcuffs while being escorted by a Captain, for whipping another Captain's ass!

This only added to the mystique of Big Fruit and #C70 Fruit!

Meanwhile in population, Hec was still in #4 Upper regulating shit, and he had his squad still chasing them #2 Upper cats around the building. Hec had one of their lil homies from their Spofford days come through, a dude named Raw, and Hec immediately put him on the squad. Raw was the lil homie from the Bronx who used to raise hell in Spofford. He had a history with Hec and Fruit, so it was only right Hec brought him in. And Raw was up in #4 Upper on the North Side with Hec holding it down and playing his position. Raw was in and out, as he went home, and came right the fuck back in a matter of weeks! And this time around, Raw landed back in #4 Upper, but on the South Side where he went and tried to get his weight up.

Raw was on the #4 Upper South Side regulating on the strength of Hec being on the other side. Hec and Raw were still cool, and dudes knew Raw was Hec lil man.

Then one day, Raw got beside himself with Hec, and Hec wild out! Hec snatched Raw lil ass up in the C Gate of #4 Upper and told that lil nigga not to play himself! Later, that evening Raw went on his Frank Tossing mission as he told Hec to suck something through the C Gate in #4 Upper! Hec went crazy! But the police made it their business not to let Hec slide up on that South Side! Besides, Raw was putting on a show to draw attention and make sure the police knew what was going on. The very next morning, they woke Hec up to let him know he was going up north! Hec copped out to a 5 to 15 on a Robbery beef for snatching a Money Bag! Hec got up that morning and straight wild out! Hec went on the South Side of #4 Upper with 2 spoiled milks in his hand. He walked up to Raw cell, woke the nigga Raw up, and tossed the spoiled milks in his face! Hec then somehow made his way down to #1 Main Bing to see Fruit before he got on that bus. Hec told Fruit about Raw, and all Fruit could do was laugh. Raw was their lil homie since their juvenile days as kids, and he couldn't believe Raw was bugging like that!

Shoe Shine
Maino

C.O Ebron w/ #1 Lower

Inf
aka
Pooching
Pretty Boy
Star

Ant (Franklin Ave)

Ant (Franklin Ave)

Eventually, Fruit ran into Raw on a visit.

With Fruit being on a one-man bubble visit, he'd seen Raw come out on the visit floor. Fruit shouted Raw out, and when he caught Raw attention, Fruit asked him what went wrong with him and Hec! Raw ain't waste no time, he immediately threw Fruit a frank, and told Fruit to suck something in front of the whole visiting room.

Fruit was in that one-man bubble going crazy because he couldn't get his hands on Raw. Next thing you know.

World, Fat Mike from Harlem and Cock Eye from Queens were all 3 being escorted out onto the visit floor and into the Bing Bubble visit.

And as they walked pass Fruit in his bubble, Fruit told World to immediately get at the nigga Raw right there on the visit! And in true fashion, World popped on Raw.

Fat Mike popped on Raw. And Cockey who had trouble seeing straight, messed around and tossed a chair in the direction of Raw's visitor!

The visiting room was in an uproar as the Squad came through and had to drag World off Raw. Then, Raw got escorted off the visit yelling and screaming at Fruit!

Once again, all eyes were on Fruit, just like they were when he tossed Fruit a frank. The police rolled up to Fruit's bubble visit and all they could do was laugh and respect how the call was made. And this beef with Raw would go on in population for months. With anyone and everyone getting at him because Fruit said the nigga was FOOD! The mystique of Big Fruit was not only enhanced with the Raw massacre, but it made Fruit the most notorious adolescent in #C74 at that time! The legend of #C70 Fruit was real! And Raw felt the wrath of Fruit! It was to the point where Raw had been cut a few times while banging out with dudes. And it began to be too much for security in the building. Raw was trying to get back at dudes and the police felt the need to try to bring it all to an end! The police made a trip to Fruit cell in #6 Lower Bing and basically begged Fruit to call the wolves off! Fruit listened, but he ain't agree to shit!

Instead, Fruit told dudes to keep riding on the nigga Raw! And that's exactly what went down for months to come in #C74 as well as HDM Bing where the adolescents were being housed! Years later, Fruit would run in to Raw in Downstate Correctional Facility on his way being transferred closer to NYC! When Fruit ran in to Raw, Fruit told that muthafuka he better had not pulled no stunt in Downstate and fuck up Fruit's transfer.

Raw was so shook, all he could do was point at all his cuts and scars on his face and tell Fruit "I don't want no more beef!" Fruit acknowledged the fact that the nigga was throwing in the white towel, and Fruit didn't press the issue. Instead, Fruit took his ass on his transfer to a facility close to NYC and never thought about Raw ever again, in the prison system!

The saga continued in the #4 Building with the Raw massacre, and Big Fruit was to blame! As Fruit laid up in #6 Lower Bing the security pulled the trigger on Fruit and damn near everyone else in the Bing who was walking around in handcuffs or who had over 90 days to serve in the Bing! It was a sunny morning in late May 93', and they packed everybody up and sent them all to HDM Bing - #1B. They created a long-term Bing for adolescents in HDM, with the adults upstairs in their Bing #1A. There were a few #C74 Alumni upstairs in #1A Bing (Shoe Shine, Lakey Da Kid, Deluxe, Germ, Puerto Rican Pete Rock and Twin from the Bronx). The #C74 Alumni were all housed upstairs in #1A Bing because they all turned adult and went to the adults on GO TIME! They were all in the Bing for cutting or stabbing a muthafuka over that jack! When the adolescents first arrived to HDM they immediately got into a major scuffle and ass whipping from the police in that build-ing! Fruit fucked around and told dudes to flood their cells to get him moved, and when the adolescents got riled up, the police came through and set niggas straight! The police whipped so much ass that day, they sent half the adolescents to KCH (Kings County Hospital). Fruit's stay in HDM was limited as he turned adult and moved on to different buildings because of his CMC status.

As Fruit sat on Rikers Island 93' summer, some of Da Boyz were up north in Coxsackie Correctional Facility waiting for his arrival.

Fruit hadn't been to trial just yet, but he was ready to get up north and do his damn time. They were playing games in the courts, and they weren't giving Fruit NO COP OUT TO NOTH-ING! Members of Da Boyz would correspond with Fruit, letting him know his bandit was there, the dude who cut Fruit on Rikers Island back in 92', and whenever he sends the word, it's lit! Fruit shouldn't have had to send NO WORD; it should have just been done! Instead, Fruit would spare Da Boyz from his wrath as he told dudes to stand down and wait for his arrival! Which came a little too late as the dude had peeled off and went to a medium security facility before Fruit landed in Coxsackie! That shit left a bad taste in Fruit mouth when it came to Da Boyz, and Hec knew it!

Once Fruit blew trial and made his way up north, he stopped at Comstock (Gladiator School) first! As soon as Fruit got off Quarantine Status and was allowed to go to the yard, he did just that because he already knew there were a few dudes there he had touched on Rikers Island back in 91'! And no sooner than Fruit arrived in the yard, he was shaking out with a dude he cut in 91', only to have to touch the nigga up again up north because the dude tried to pull a move on Fruit in Comstock yard. The dude did himself a disservice by trying

to get at Fruit!

Not only was he disap-pointed again, but he also landed on keep lock status with the comrade Inf aka Pooching from Fort Greene! Inf and fruit had history. In fact, Inf was with Fruit when Fruit cut the shit out of the dude the first time, back in 91 when they were in #3 Lower! Inf couldn't believe the nigga pulled a stunt on Fruity! Inf regulated the keep-lock recreation one day, and made sure he was able to get up on the dude. And sure enough: Loyal To A Fault – Inf touched the nigga again, this time it was for Fruit!

The incident pushed Fruit to Coxsackie on keeplock status. Fruit got off keeplock after 30 days, and when he touched population, it was like being in #C74 all over again!

Once there were a few of Da Boyz in Coxsackie (Fruit, Hec, Ron Mack, Deluxe and Sha aka Saquan) they got back on their bully! Only this time, there were a few hitters to join the click! Moe Dog was in the building, and he had his man Fangz from Brownsville with him, as well as Little Nitty! Black Kassem from ENY and a few Fort Greene dudes were on deck as well! Coxsackie wasn't just #C74 all over again, the shit was a damn fashion show every day in the yard and on the chow line! Dudes were changing their clothes two or three times a day, and that led to a whole lot of heist going on because dudes had stay jigged! It also let Fruit know that this wasn't the spot for him.

He knew he had time to serve, and doing it in Coxsackie like that, wasn't going to make it! One day Fruit and Moe Dog were hitting the pull up bar, and a voice came out the second-floor window, calling Fruit name from Reception! Fruit ignored the voice at first, telling the dude he didn't know who he was!

Mass of tears

**...ILL
...STATTER**

...y would have
...uble at his fu-

...y tears and so
..., "Pat would
sented all of us
...priest and fam-
...old a crush of
...ing their last
...rday to the ded-
...ok school prin-

...nt down by a
...ast week when
...nto the middle
...le at the Red
...projects.

...have wanted
...lier," the Rev.
...nta told family
...dents and fel-
...rs from Red
...e School 15.
...ins; Schools
...aseph Fernan-
...city leaders.
...cked into Our
...f Peace Church
...ind, across the
...e crime-ridden
using project
...8, lost his life
as he searched
ho had left his

of the bearded,
educator sent
through a city
...ed to deaths by

p and several

priests celebrated a Mass of
Christian Burial for him, two
more teenage suspects — Jermaine Russell and Khary
Bekka, both 18 — were
charged with Daly's murder.
Seventeen-year-old Shamel
Burroughs, a school dropout
and self-styled tough guy, was
charged on Friday.

An overflow crowd of 500,
including hundreds of school
administrators wearing
black-lapel ribbons, jammed
into the small church in the
New Dorp section while at
least 1,000 more people stood
outside, under a pale winter
sun.

Hundreds of PS 15 pupils
and relatives, bused across
the Verrazano Bridge, listened from the church base-
ment to the service, conduct-
ed by Bishop Patrick Ahern
of the New York Archdio-
cese. He was assisted by Garaventa, a cousin of Daly's
wife, Madeline.

The couple has twin daugh-
ters and a son.

"What doth the Lord re-
quire of thee, but to do justly,
and to love kindness, and to
walk humbly with thy God,"
Garaventa quoted from the
book of Micah 6.8. "I am not
sure if Pat's eyes ever lighted
on these words, but we know
deep within our hearts Pat
Daly was such a man."

Daly, a teacher and admin-
istrator at PS 15 for 26 years,
was known to two genera-

SUSPECTS in slaying of principal Patrick Daly are Khary Bekka of
Brooklyn (l.) and Jermaine Russell of S.I.   DENNIS CARUSO Daily News

tions of local residents as the
Mayor of Red Hook, or Mr. D.,
but Garaventa said he "never
dwelt on his goodness, he
never trumpeted it."

As the service concluded, a
procession with pupils from
Daly's school and their par-
ents walked by the coffin to
say their final farewells.

Some clutched his picture
in their hands, many sobbed
and wiped away tears.

"Everyone's dying there,"
Quann Braxton, 13, one of the
slain man's pupils said of life
in the Red Hook projects.
"First my brother was shot,
then my grandmother, now
Mr. Daly."

Daly slay: Guilty
3 convicted of murdering principal

Execute 'em, say Red Hook moms

Then, the dude said his government name, and it turned out to be Big Nut from LG passing through Coxsackie after shaking it up across the street at Greene Correctional Facility! Nut was still cocked up on swoll, and he hit that steele in the yard and gym like it was nothing! As most dudes were impressed, some dudes were envious and even jealous. Something Nut was used to! It eventually led to Nut straight smashing a nigga with his bare hands to the point where it wasn't considered just a fist fight! Big Nut had to go! Nut was on his way up to Barehill Correctional Facility, where he would flex on niggas, cocked up, wearing Coochie Sweaters and Gator Shoes on visits, until he slid back to the streets in 94/95'. Big Nut was the illest, for real! Tito was one of a kind!

After Nut slid up out of Coxsackie Fruit didn't last much longer.

Fruit got flagged for a cutting and a razor in his cell and joined a whole crew of muthafukas serving keeplock in Coxsackie over in E and F Block.

He joined Moe Dog and Lil Nitty for a minute before taking his show on the road to South Port Correctional Facility (Special Housing Unit), where he would run into Pretty Boy Star from LG, and they would have to straighten some things out! Pretty Boy Star was the first baby father to Fruit's victim. And it was an awkward situation for the two of them.

Especially, since Pretty Boy slandered Fruit's name and got a whole bunch of muthafukas up north and in South Port all riled up! They had the chance to speak through vents and sink holes, but they never got up on each other. Fruit eventually slid to Clinton Correctional Facility, where he began to serve real time and man up!

When he landed in the spot, there were a whole lot of OGs in the building, and Fruit had to learn quick, who was who and what was what in that prison!

There were a few Comrades there as well (Rondu, Wink and Money from Brownsville, Drak from ENY, Ant from Franklin Ave and Big Sharky James aka Big Sha from Bedstuy) so the transition for Fruit was cool. And after two or three months in that spot, Fruit walked into the Messhall one morning, only to see Moe Dog, Vardo and Little Nitty fresh from Coxsackie! The squad let it be known that Big Belly Man Hec got cut, and they blew the roof off Coxsackie! When Hec got cut by a Muslim dude in Coxsackie, it was lit! With the General Moe Dog in the building, everyone waited for his call. Not only was he the General, but Dog was also Muslim!

Well, Dog is wired different and he's a General for real! So, Dog let it be known that the North Yard in Coxsackie was gonna be the spot where it goes down.

And sure enough, the next morning, Dog went out to the

North Yard and stepped straight to his business for Big Belly Man Hec! Dog was putting that knife work in, and everyone else followed! It was a full-blown riot in that North Yard that morning as the Comrades revenged Hec's cutting! Dudes were transferred and moved all over the state behind that bang out! Fruit even ran into Black Kassem in Clinton one day being escorted into E Block (Long Term Keeplock) because Kaseem was caught up in the bang out as well. Fruit wished he could have been there holding it down with and for Big Belly Man Hec wherever they were because Hec was his BROTHER!...

So, at Clinton Correctional Facility, Fruit was off and running, about to make his mark up north in them mountains. The year was 1994 and Fruit would go on to serve another 20 more years before being released back into society in 2014!

Up Next : Da Boyz To Men (Life After Incarceration)
feat : Big Fruit, Black Mick, Moe Dog, Maino, Germ,
Pee Wee, Moe Joe, Vardo and BK Moe aka Reese
Written By : Fruitquan Bailey

ACKNOWLEDGMENTS

Special Thanks and Acknowledgements: I want to Thank my Beautiful Wife (Queen Sunni) for putting up with all my nonsense while writing this book and being that rock and support I always need. You're the best Momma! I want to Thank my dad (Big Fruitquan) for passing me his undeniable talent and skill of writing. I also want to Thank Da Boyz for allowing me to go through my mental rolodex, reminisce and bring forth some classic memories of our youth and adolescence, both good and bad! Our time spent on Rikers Island #C74 was a traumatizing experience for us all, and I'm proud to know that most of us have prevailed and overcome the obstacles set in our paths due to our own choices and decisions. I want to Thank all of my Social Media and YouTube supporters for their continuous

support! Without you guys, I doubt if I would have ever written any of the stories, I've brought forth to the streets! I want to Thank the Streets and all the Hoods across the U.S that listen to and watch my platforms in the Barbershops, Beauty Salons, Pool Halls and Gambling Spots!... This one right here was for The Comrades!

Rest In Peace : Big Belly Man Hec, Shamel aka Lil Hec, Nut aka Tito, Shoe Shine, Kojak, Rome, Inf aka Poo Ching, Fly Ty, Chyna (Connecticut), Lil Goggy, Popcorn, O.P, Kendeer, T-Roy, Alpo (Queens)

Kay
Russ

Fruit
Butter
Fruit

IN LOVING MEMORY OF
JUANITA REYES
JUNE 20, 1914 — OCT 24, 1994
HECTOR PACHECO
OCT 14, 1946 — MAY 1996
Shamel (Son) : RIP
Hec (Dad) : RIP

6
Maino #1 Main Bing

Maino : His Old Cell

Maino : Feel His Pain

Vardo
Just
Killa
Rumble
FG/67

Miz
Fruit
Lil Tah
Emel
Maino

Dorian
Joe
Moe

Puerto Rican Phil

Germ
&
Rondu

Pito

#C74 Alumni

Fruit
Loso aka KC

Mouse
Fruit
Leon